Phonics Tales! ™

th

The Thing That Went Thump

by Maria Fleming

illustrated by Stephen Lewis

SCHOLASTIC INC.

New York • Toronto • London • Auckland • Sydney
Mexico City • New Delhi • Hong Kong • Buenos Aires

One **Thursday** night, **Theo Thorn** was very sleepy.

Phonics Fact

The digraph *th* can also appear at the end of a word, as in **bath** and **teeth**.

So **Theo** took a **bath**, brushed his **teeth**, and went to bed early.

Suddenly, **Theo** heard a strange sound.
Thump! Thump! Thud! Thump! Thump! Thud!

What could it be? **Theo thought** of a **thousand** scary **things**.

Maybe it was a giant **sloth with thick** fur.
Thump! Thump! Thud!

Maybe it was a wooly **mammoth with** big **teeth**.
Thump! Thump! Thud!

Maybe it was a monster **with three** heads and **thirty** eyes. **Thump**! **Thump**! **Thud**!

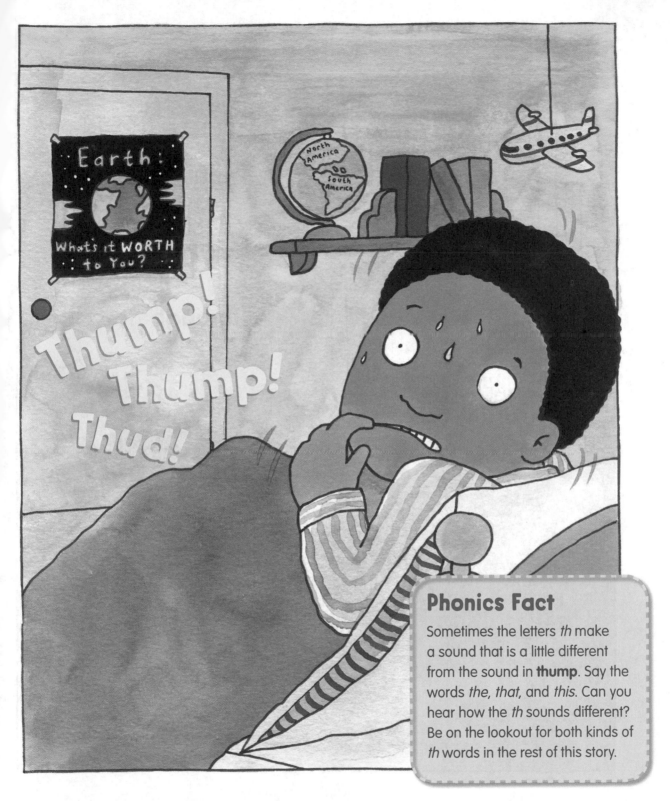

Phonics Fact

Sometimes the letters *th* make a sound that is a little different from the sound in **thump**. Say the words *the*, *that*, and *this*. Can you hear how the *th* sounds different? Be on the lookout for both kinds of *th* words in the rest of this story.

THUMP! THUMP! THUD! THUMP! THUMP! THUD!
The **thumping thing** was getting closer!

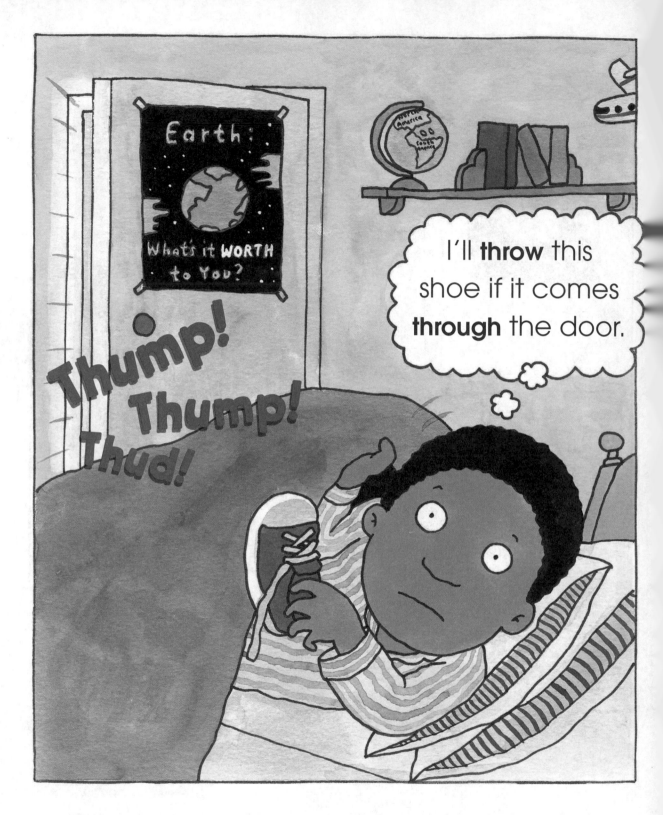

Theo hid **beneath** the covers. He held his **breath**. Suddenly, the door burst open. In **thumped**…

...**Theo's** sister!

"**Ruth**, you scared me to **death**!" said **Theo**.

"Sorry, **Theo**," said **Ruth**. "Will you help me **with** my **math** homework?"

"Okay," said **Theo**.
Theo was **thankful** the **thumping thing**
was only his sister.

But he made **Ruth** take an **oath** that she would never scare him like that again.

TH Riddles

Listen to the riddles. Then match each with the right *th* word from the box. (Hint: Sometimes the *th* appears at the end of the word.)

Word Box

Earth	thump	sloth	thorn	bath
Thursday	three	teeth	math	thick

1. This day comes after Wednesday.

2. This is something very pointy.

3. You need these to chew food.

4. This is the opposite of *thin*.

5. This is the planet we live on.

6. This animal moves very slowly.

7. You take this to get clean.

8. You use numbers to do this subject.

9. This loud sound rhymes with *bump*.

10. This number comes after *two*.

TH Cheer

Hooray for *t-h*, the best sound around!

Let's holler *t-h* words all over town!

There's **thump** and **thing** and **teeth** and **mouth**.

There's **thumb** and **thorn** and **north** and **south**.

There's **thread** and **throat** and **bath** and **moth**.

There's **think** and **thank** and **math** and **cloth**.

T-h, *t-h*, give a great cheer,

For the most **thrilling** sound you ever will hear!

Make a list of other words that have *th* at the beginning or the end. Then use them in your cheer.